The Energy Key

The Energy Key

Matthew Petchinsky

The Energy Key: Unlocking Limitless Motivation
By: Matthew Petchinsky

Introduction

Energy is the lifeblood of human motivation, the invisible force that propels us toward our dreams, aspirations, and goals. It is what fuels our actions, shapes our thoughts, and drives our emotions. Without energy, even the most ambitious plans falter, and the brightest of dreams can dim. Whether physical, mental, or emotional, energy plays a pivotal role in determining the quality of our lives and our ability to achieve greatness.

However, energy is not a static resource; it is dynamic and can be cultivated, aligned, and optimized. In today's fast-paced world, where demands on our time and attention are greater than ever, understanding and harnessing the power of energy is no longer a luxury—it's a necessity. The concept of limitless motivation is not about chasing fleeting bursts of inspiration but rather about sustaining a steady, powerful flow of energy that fuels consistent progress and achievement.

At its core, motivation stems from the alignment of physical, mental, and emotional energy. Physical energy is the foundation, derived from our health, nutrition, and activity levels. Mental energy shapes our focus, clarity, and the ability to think critically and creatively. Emotional energy, often overlooked, governs our resilience, relationships, and the passion that drives us forward. When these three elements are out of balance, we feel drained, unproductive, and overwhelmed. But when they are aligned, we unlock our limitless potential and achieve more than we ever thought possible.

This book is your guide to mastering the art of energy alignment and maintaining high levels of motivation. It is not a collection of empty platitudes or overly simplistic advice but a practical and actionable roadmap for real, lasting change. Each chapter delves into strategies that are grounded in science and experience, designed to help you harness your energy effectively. You will discover how to:

- Optimize physical energy through effective habits, diet, and movement.
- Enhance mental clarity and focus to cut through distractions and maintain momentum.
- Build emotional resilience and channel passion to overcome obstacles and maintain drive.

The principles in this book are timeless, meaning they can be applied at any stage of life or circumstance. Whether you are a student striving for academic success, a professional seeking career advancement, or an individual pursuing personal fulfillment, the strategies shared here will empower you to stay motivated, energized, and aligned with your purpose.

By the time you reach the final page, you will have a comprehensive toolkit for not just understanding energy but mastering it. You will be equipped with the knowledge and techniques to maintain peak motivation, even in the face of challenges. This book is not merely a guide; it is an invitation to transform your life by unlocking the limitless energy that lies within you.

Are you ready to harness your full potential and fuel your journey with boundless motivation? Let's begin.

Chapter 1: The Science of Energy and Motivation

Energy and motivation are deeply intertwined, forming the foundation of human behavior. At the crossroads of neuroscience and psychology lies the answer to why some days we feel unstoppable while on others, even the simplest tasks feel insurmountable. Understanding the biological and psychological underpinnings of energy and motivation is key to unlocking sustained drive and achieving our goals.

This chapter delves into the science behind energy and motivation, focusing on the critical roles played by neurotransmitters, hormones, and daily habits. By understanding these mechanisms, we can make informed choices to optimize our energy levels and, in turn, maintain high levels of motivation.

The Relationship Between Energy and Motivation

Motivation is often thought of as a mental phenomenon, but it is deeply rooted in biological processes. At its core, motivation is a state that arises when the brain perceives a gap between the current state and a desired outcome. Energy, on the other hand, is the fuel that enables action to close this gap.

From a neurological perspective, the brain prioritizes tasks based on the availability of energy. When energy levels are high, the brain can efficiently allocate resources to focus, plan, and execute actions. Conversely, when energy is low, the brain prioritizes conservation, often leading to procrastination or a lack of motivation.

The cycle of energy and motivation is self-reinforcing: high energy fuels motivation, and motivation drives behaviors that replenish or maintain energy. However, disruptions in this cycle—due to stress, poor habits, or environmental factors—can lead to energy depletion and diminished drive.

The Role of Neurotransmitters and Hormones in Motivation

The brain's chemistry plays a pivotal role in regulating energy and motivation. Several key neurotransmitters and hormones act as chemical messengers, influencing how we feel, think, and act. Let's explore the primary players:

1. **Dopamine: The Reward Molecule**

   Dopamine is often referred to as the "feel-good" neurotransmitter, but its role extends far beyond pleasure. It is crucial for reward-based motivation and goal-directed behavior. Dopamine surges when we anticipate achieving something rewarding, creating a sense of drive and focus.

   - **How it works:** When you set a goal and envision its completion, dopamine levels increase, encouraging you to take action.
   - **Optimizing dopamine:** Engage in activities that offer small, frequent rewards, such as breaking larger goals into manageable steps. Celebrate progress to maintain momentum.

2. **Serotonin: The Mood Stabilizer**

   Serotonin regulates mood, emotion, and overall well-being. A balanced serotonin level promotes a sense of calm and optimism, both of which are essential for sustained motivation.

   - **How it works:** Serotonin is associated with feelings of contentment and confidence, reducing the emotional burden of setbacks.
   - **Optimizing serotonin:** Exposure to sunlight, regular exercise, and practicing gratitude can naturally boost serotonin levels.

3. **Cortisol: The Stress Hormone**

Cortisol is a double-edged sword. In small amounts, it provides the energy and alertness needed to respond to challenges. However, chronic stress can lead to elevated cortisol levels, draining energy and suppressing motivation.

- **How it works:** Cortisol triggers the fight-or-flight response, diverting energy to immediate survival rather than long-term goals.
- **Managing cortisol:** Incorporate stress-reduction techniques such as mindfulness, deep breathing, and sufficient sleep to maintain healthy cortisol levels.

Identifying Energy Leaks in Your Daily Routine

Energy leaks are habits, behaviors, or environmental factors that drain your physical, mental, or emotional energy without providing meaningful returns. Identifying and addressing these leaks is crucial for sustaining motivation.

1. **Physical Energy Leaks**
   - **Lack of sleep:** Sleep deprivation reduces cognitive function, emotional regulation, and physical stamina.
   - **Poor nutrition:** Diets high in processed foods and sugar can lead to energy crashes.
   - **Sedentary lifestyle:** Physical inactivity reduces circulation and energy levels.

Quick Fixes:

-
   - Aim for 7–8 hours of quality sleep per night.
   - Incorporate balanced meals with protein, healthy fats, and complex carbohydrates.
   - Add movement breaks to your day, such as stretching or walking.

2.Mental Energy Leaks

- **Decision fatigue:** Making too many decisions depletes mental energy.
- **Multitasking:** Dividing attention reduces efficiency and focus.
- **Digital distractions:** Constant notifications and screen time overstimulate the brain.

Quick Fixes:

- Simplify choices by creating routines and habits.
- Prioritize single-tasking over multitasking for better focus.
- Designate tech-free periods to recharge your mental energy.

3.Emotional Energy Leaks

- **Negative relationships:** Toxic interactions drain emotional reserves.
- **Unresolved stress:** Suppressed worries or anxieties consume energy.
- **Lack of boundaries:** Overcommitting leaves little energy for personal needs.

Quick Fixes:

- Surround yourself with supportive and uplifting people.

- Practice journaling or talking through challenges to process emotions.
- Learn to say no to commitments that do not align with your goals.

The Path Forward

Understanding the science of energy and motivation is the first step toward creating meaningful and lasting change in your life. By aligning your physical, mental, and emotional energy, you can overcome obstacles, achieve your goals, and sustain a level of motivation that feels effortless and natural.

Chapter 2: Building Your Personal Energy Bank

Energy is the currency of life. Just as a bank account requires deposits to grow, your personal energy bank requires consistent replenishment to sustain motivation and drive. Building and maintaining a robust energy reserve begins with understanding the different types of energy—physical, mental, emotional, and spiritual—and learning how to nurture each one. In this chapter, we'll explore how to cultivate these energy types, maintain balance, and implement daily habits and rituals to keep your reserves full and thriving.

The Four Types of Energy

Each type of energy contributes uniquely to your overall well-being and productivity. A balanced energy bank ensures that you have the resources to meet life's demands and pursue your goals with vigor and clarity.

1. **Physical Energy**

   The foundation of all other energy types, physical energy is derived from your body's vitality and health. It powers your actions and ensures your brain and body function optimally.
   - **Sources:** Sleep, nutrition, hydration, and movement.
   - **Signs of depletion:** Fatigue, sluggishness, frequent illness, or lack of stamina.

2. **Mental Energy**

   Mental energy governs your ability to focus, solve problems, and make decisions. It determines how well you can manage cognitive tasks and remain productive.
   - **Sources:** Clarity, focus, and mental stimulation.
   - **Signs of depletion:** Brain fog, indecision, difficulty concentrating, or feeling overwhelmed.

3. **Emotional Energy**

Emotional energy influences your resilience, relationships, and ability to maintain a positive outlook. It fuels empathy, passion, and joy.

- **Sources:** Healthy relationships, self-care, and emotional regulation.
- **Signs of depletion:** Irritability, apathy, mood swings, or feeling emotionally drained.

4. **Spiritual Energy**

Spiritual energy connects you to your purpose, values, and a sense of meaning. It fuels your sense of direction and provides inner peace.

- **Sources:** Mindfulness, meditation, nature, and alignment with your values.
- **Signs of depletion:** Feeling lost, purposeless, or disconnected.

Techniques for Cultivating and Maintaining Each Energy Type

Building your energy bank requires intentional habits and practices. Below are techniques tailored to each energy type to help you cultivate and maintain balance.

1. **Physical Energy Techniques**
   - **Prioritize Sleep:** Aim for 7–9 hours of quality sleep each night. Create a bedtime routine, limit screen time before bed, and ensure your sleep environment is comfortable.
   - **Nourish Your Body:** Eat a balanced diet rich in whole foods. Focus on protein, complex carbohydrates, healthy fats, and micronutrients. Avoid excessive sugar and processed foods.
   - **Stay Active:** Incorporate regular exercise into your routine, such as walking, yoga, or strength training. Even short bursts of movement can boost energy.
   - **Hydrate:** Dehydration can sap energy. Aim for at least 8 glasses of water daily and adjust based on your activity level.
2. **Mental Energy Techniques**
   - **Practice Mindfulness:** Spend a few minutes each day focusing on your breath or observing your thoughts without judgment. Mindfulness improves mental clarity and reduces stress.
   - **Organize Your Tasks:** Use tools like to-do lists, planners, or apps to manage your workload. Prioritize tasks based on urgency and importance.

- **Take Mental Breaks:** Follow techniques like the Pomodoro method (25 minutes of focused work followed by a 5-minute break) to prevent burnout.
- **Learn and Stimulate:** Engage in activities that challenge your brain, such as reading, puzzles, or learning new skills.

3. **Emotional Energy Techniques**

- **Express Gratitude:** Spend time each day reflecting on things you are grateful for. Gratitude shifts focus from negativity to positivity, replenishing emotional reserves.
- **Cultivate Relationships:** Nurture connections with supportive friends and family. Limit time with people who drain your energy.
- **Engage in Self-Care:** Dedicate time to activities that bring you joy, whether it's reading, taking a bath, or enjoying a hobby.
- **Manage Emotions:** Journaling, therapy, or talking to a trusted confidant can help process emotions and release tension.

4. **Spiritual Energy Techniques**

- **Meditate:** Regular meditation helps you connect with your inner self and fosters a sense of peace.
- **Align with Purpose:** Reflect on your core values and ensure your daily actions align with them. Doing meaningful work nourishes spiritual energy.
- **Spend Time in Nature:** Connecting with the natural world can provide perspective and a sense of renewal.
- **Practice Stillness:** Take moments of silence to reflect and listen to your inner thoughts.

Daily Habits and Rituals to Replenish Energy Reserves

Incorporating intentional habits into your daily routine can prevent energy depletion and ensure your reserves remain full. Here's a blueprint for cultivating daily rituals:

1. **Morning Routine:**
    - Start your day with hydration by drinking a glass of water.
    - Engage in a quick movement routine, such as stretching or yoga, to awaken your body.
    - Set an intention for the day to align with your purpose.

2. **Midday Check-In:**
    - Pause to evaluate your energy levels. Are you feeling drained or focused? Adjust accordingly.
    - Incorporate a mindfulness practice, such as deep breathing or a short walk, to recharge.
    - Refuel with a nutritious meal or snack that balances protein, fats, and carbs.

3. **Evening Wind-Down:**
    - Reflect on your day by journaling about achievements or moments of gratitude.
    - Unplug from screens at least 30 minutes before bedtime to prepare your mind for rest.
    - Practice relaxation techniques, such as reading or meditation, to ease into sleep.

4. **Weekly Rituals:**
    - Dedicate time to activities that bring joy and fulfillment, such as hobbies or socializing.
    - Engage in a larger reflection, asking what went well and where adjustments are needed.

- Plan for the upcoming week to reduce stress and foster clarity.

Building Momentum in Your Energy Bank

Replenishing your energy reserves is not a one-time effort but a continuous process. By consistently practicing these habits and techniques, you'll find that your energy bank not only stabilizes but grows over time. This surplus of energy becomes a wellspring that fuels your motivation and enables you to face challenges with resilience and enthusiasm.

Chapter 3: Mastering Energy Flow for Peak Performance

Energy flow is the seamless connection between energy availability, focus, and action. When energy flows optimally, tasks feel effortless, productivity soars, and creativity thrives. This state, often described as being "in the zone" or achieving "flow," is the hallmark of peak performance. However, energy flow is not accidental—it requires intentional management of time, tasks, and energy reserves.

This chapter introduces the concept of energy flow, explores time management techniques to align your peak energy with critical tasks, and provides strategies for overcoming common energy blocks like procrastination and burnout. By mastering energy flow, you can elevate your performance and sustain high levels of motivation and productivity.

What Is Energy Flow?

Energy flow is the state in which your physical, mental, and emotional energy align harmoniously to support focused and purposeful action. This state is not simply about being active; it is about being effective. Energy flow allows you to:

- Enter a state of deep focus where distractions fade away.
- Tap into creativity and problem-solving abilities with ease.
- Sustain effort and momentum over long periods without feeling drained.

Energy flow is the foundation of peak performance. It is the difference between working hard and working smart, allowing you to maximize results while minimizing wasted effort.

Achieving Energy Flow

To achieve energy flow, you must align your energy levels with your tasks, ensuring that high-priority activities are undertaken when your energy is at its peak. This requires an understanding of your personal energy rhythms and the ability to structure your day accordingly.

1. **Identify Your Peak Energy Times**

   Everyone has natural energy rhythms, influenced by factors like sleep patterns, nutrition, and environment. These rhythms, often referred to as your circadian rhythm, dictate when you feel most alert and when your energy dips.
   - **Morning people:** Peak energy occurs early in the day.
   - **Night owls:** Energy surges later in the evening.
   - **Midday performers:** Energy is balanced, with peaks around mid-morning and early afternoon.

Action Step: Track your energy levels for a week, noting when you feel most focused and productive. Use this information to schedule high-priority tasks during peak times.

2.Eliminate Energy Distractions

Energy flow requires an environment that supports focus. Identify and minimize distractions, such as:

- Notifications on your phone or computer.
- Cluttered workspaces that impede mental clarity.
- Multitasking, which divides attention and reduces efficiency.

Action Step: Create a dedicated workspace, set boundaries for interruptions, and use tools like focus timers or noise-canceling headphones to enhance concentration.

Time Management Techniques to Align Energy with Tasks

Effective time management is crucial for aligning energy flow with key tasks. By structuring your day around your energy rhythms, you can optimize performance and avoid unnecessary stress.

1. **The Time-Energy Matrix**

   Use a matrix to categorize tasks based on their energy requirements and urgency:
   - **High Energy + High Priority:** Schedule during peak energy times.
   - **Low Energy + High Priority:** Simplify or delegate.
   - **High Energy + Low Priority:** Batch or defer.
   - **Low Energy + Low Priority:** Eliminate or minimize.

Action Step: At the start of each week, map your tasks into the matrix and plan accordingly.

1. **The 80/20 Rule (Pareto Principle)**

   Focus on the 20% of tasks that produce 80% of your results. By prioritizing high-impact activities, you maximize productivity and conserve energy.

   Action Step: Identify your "big wins" for the day and tackle them first.

2. **Time Blocking**

   Divide your day into blocks dedicated to specific activities. This prevents decision fatigue and ensures focused energy for each task.

   Action Step: Create blocks for deep work, administrative tasks, and relaxation to maintain balance.

3. **Task Batching**

   Group similar tasks together to reduce the mental load of context switching. For example, respond to emails in one session rather than throughout the day.

Action Step: Designate time for recurring tasks like emails, meetings, and planning.

Action Step: Designate time for recurring tasks like emails, meetings, and planning.

Overcoming Energy Blocks

Energy blocks, such as procrastination and burnout, disrupt energy flow and hinder performance. Addressing these blocks requires both prevention and intervention strategies.

1. **Procrastination**

   Procrastination often arises from fear of failure, perfectionism, or lack of clarity. It saps energy and creates unnecessary stress.
   - **Break tasks into smaller steps:** Overwhelming tasks can be tackled more easily when divided into manageable chunks.
   - **Use the 2-Minute Rule:** Commit to starting a task for just two minutes. Often, this initial action generates momentum to continue.
   - **Reward progress:** Use small rewards to reinforce effort and build motivation.

2. **Burnout**

   Burnout occurs when prolonged stress depletes your physical, mental, and emotional energy. It leads to disengagement, reduced performance, and exhaustion.
   - **Recognize early signs:** Symptoms include chronic fatigue, irritability, and declining motivation.
   - **Prioritize rest and recovery:** Incorporate regular breaks, vacations, and hobbies to recharge.
   - **Set boundaries:** Learn to say no to unnecessary commitments and protect your energy.

3. **Overcoming Stagnation**

   At times, you may feel stuck or uninspired, unable to regain energy flow.
   - **Change your environment:** A new setting can spark creativity and refresh your mindset.
   - **Engage in energy-boosting activities:** Physical exercise, a creative hobby, or even a brief walk can reignite energy.
   - **Revisit your purpose:** Reflect on your goals and motivations to reconnect with what drives you.

Building Sustainable Energy Flow

Achieving energy flow is not a one-time effort but a dynamic process that evolves with your needs and circumstances. The key to sustaining energy flow lies in balancing effort with recovery, staying adaptable, and continually refining your approach to time and energy management.

1. **Daily Flow Rituals:**

   Create rituals that anchor your energy flow throughout the day. Examples include morning mindfulness, midday check-ins, and evening reflections.

2. **Weekly Flow Reviews:**

   Dedicate time each week to assess your energy flow and identify areas for improvement.

3. **Celebrate Progress:**

   Acknowledge your achievements, no matter how small, to reinforce positive energy flow and motivation.

The Path to Peak Performance

Mastering energy flow transforms how you approach your goals. By aligning your tasks with your peak energy and proactively addressing energy blocks, you can achieve sustained peak performance. As you integrate these techniques into your routine, you will find yourself not just working harder but working smarter, fueled by a steady and powerful flow of energy.

Chapter 4: Motivation on Demand: Triggering Your Inner Power

Motivation is often perceived as a fleeting emotion, something we must wait for to accomplish great things. But what if motivation could be summoned on demand? By understanding the psychological and emotional levers that drive action, you can create personalized triggers to ignite your inner power whenever needed. In this chapter, we will explore how to use anchors and affirmations, visualization techniques, and the power of small wins to cultivate a consistent, renewable source of motivation.

Creating Personalized Motivation Triggers Using Anchors and Affirmations

Motivation triggers are cues or signals that evoke a specific emotional or mental state. Anchors and affirmations are two powerful tools for establishing these triggers.

What Are Anchors?

Anchors are external or internal stimuli that link to a particular emotional or physical response. For example, hearing a specific song might remind you of a triumphant moment, instantly boosting your mood and energy. By intentionally creating anchors, you can train your brain to associate certain cues with feelings of motivation.

Steps to Create Motivation Anchors:

1. **Identify a Powerful State:** Reflect on a time when you felt highly motivated, confident, or energized. Relive the moment in your mind, focusing on the emotions, physical sensations, and thoughts.

2. **Choose a Trigger:** Select a specific action or stimulus to associate with this state. Common triggers include:
   - Touching a specific point on your body, such as pressing your thumb and forefinger together.
   - Hearing a specific word or phrase.
   - Playing a particular song or sound.
3. **Reinforce the Connection:** While immersed in the feeling of motivation, perform the chosen action or expose yourself to the stimulus repeatedly. The stronger the emotional state during this process, the stronger the anchor will become.
4. **Activate the Anchor:** Use the trigger whenever you need a boost of motivation. Over time, your brain will respond automatically, recreating the desired state.

Affirmations for Motivation

Affirmations are positive, empowering statements designed to re-shape your mindset and self-belief. When repeated consistently, they can override limiting beliefs and cultivate a motivation-ready mindset.

Examples of Motivational Affirmations:

- "I am unstoppable, and I achieve my goals with ease."
- "Every small step I take brings me closer to success."
- "I am full of energy and ready to tackle any challenge."

How to Use Affirmations Effectively:

1. **Personalize Your Affirmations:** Tailor them to your goals and values. Specific, emotionally resonant affirmations are more impactful than generic ones.
2. **Repeat Daily:** Say your affirmations aloud every morning or write them down in a journal. The more you engage with them, the more ingrained they become.
3. **Pair with Visualization:** Combine affirmations with mental imagery to deepen their impact. For example, visualize yourself achieving a goal as you repeat, "I am capable and determined."

Visualization Exercises to Supercharge Motivation

Visualization is a mental rehearsal technique that involves imagining yourself achieving a desired outcome. It engages the brain's sensory and emotional systems, creating a sense of anticipation and readiness that fuels motivation.

Why Visualization Works

The brain responds to vivid mental imagery as if it were real. Visualization activates the same neural pathways used during actual performance, helping to build confidence, focus, and emotional resilience.

Exercise 1: The Success Scenario

1. **Set the Scene:** Choose a specific goal or task you want to accomplish. Close your eyes and imagine yourself in the process of achieving it.
2. **Engage Your Senses:** Include as many sensory details as possible. What do you see, hear, feel, smell, or even taste in this moment of success?
3. **Feel the Emotions:** Focus on the pride, joy, and excitement you would feel upon achieving your goal. Let these emotions flood your mind and body.
4. **Replay Regularly:** Practice this visualization daily, especially before taking action toward your goal.

Exercise 2: Overcoming Obstacles

1. **Identify Challenges:** Think of potential obstacles that could derail your progress.
2. **Visualize Solutions:** Imagine yourself overcoming each obstacle with confidence and creativity. Focus on how you feel as you navigate these challenges successfully.
3. **Anchor the Feeling:** Pair this visualization with an anchor (e.g., a physical gesture) to reinforce the sense of empowerment.

Exercise 3: Daily Motivation Booster

1. **Morning Visualization:** Spend five minutes each morning visualizing the day ahead, focusing on tasks you want to complete and how great you will feel once they are done.
2. **Evening Reflection:** Before bed, visualize the long-term impact of your daily actions, reinforcing their importance and motivating yourself for the next day.

Leveraging Small Wins to Build Momentum

Small wins are incremental achievements that create a sense of progress and build momentum. Each small victory releases dopamine, the brain's reward chemical, which reinforces positive behavior and motivates further action.

Why Small Wins Matter

- They make large goals feel attainable by breaking them into manageable steps.
- They boost confidence and reduce overwhelm.
- They create a positive feedback loop, where success leads to more success.

Strategies for Harnessing Small Wins

1. **Set Micro-Goals:** Break larger goals into smaller, actionable steps. For example, instead of "Write a book," aim for "Write 500 words today."
2. **Track Your Progress:** Use a journal, app, or checklist to record your accomplishments. Seeing your progress builds a sense of achievement and motivates you to keep going.
3. **Celebrate Success:** Reward yourself for completing each step, no matter how small. Rewards can be as simple as taking a short break, treating yourself to a favorite snack, or sharing your success with a friend.
4. **Start With Easy Wins:** Begin your day with tasks you can complete quickly and successfully. This creates an early sense of momentum that carries into more challenging tasks.

Compounding Small Wins

Small wins may seem insignificant in isolation, but their cumulative effect can be transformative. By consistently building on small victories, you develop habits, resilience, and a track record of success that propels you toward your larger goals.

Example: If your goal is to run a marathon, your small wins might include:

- Week 1: Running for 10 minutes a day.
- Week 2: Running for 15 minutes a day.
- Week 3: Completing your first 5K.

Over time, these incremental achievements lead to the ultimate victory of completing the marathon.

Bringing It All Together

Motivation on demand is not a matter of luck or waiting for inspiration to strike. It is a skill that can be cultivated through intentional practices. By creating personalized triggers, using visualization to fuel your drive, and leveraging small wins to maintain momentum, you can summon motivation whenever you need it.

Incorporate these strategies into your daily routine, and you'll find that motivation becomes a constant companion rather than a fleeting visitor.

Chapter 5: Sustaining Limitless Energy and Motivation

Motivation and energy are not static; they ebb and flow like tides, influenced by internal rhythms and external circumstances. While short bursts of motivation can drive immediate action, sustaining limitless energy and motivation requires a deeper understanding of energy cycles, strategies for navigating setbacks, and the creation of a supportive environment. In this chapter, we will explore these concepts and provide actionable insights to help you maintain your drive for the long haul.

Understanding Energy Cycles and Navigating Them Effectively

Every individual operates within natural energy cycles that influence physical, mental, and emotional performance. These cycles, governed by biological and psychological factors, can either enhance or hinder your motivation depending on how you manage them.

Types of Energy Cycles

1. **Circadian Rhythms (Daily Cycles):**
   - Governed by the body's internal clock, circadian rhythms dictate energy peaks and troughs over a 24-hour period.
   - **Peak Times:** Morning or early afternoon for most people.
   - **Troughs:** Mid-afternoon and late evening.
2. **Ultradian Rhythms (Short Cycles):**
   - Cycles of 90–120 minutes during which energy builds and then wanes.
   - **Optimal Work Periods:** Energy is highest at the start of the cycle; breaks are needed as it wanes.
3. **Seasonal Cycles:**
   - Motivation and energy can also fluctuate with the seasons, influenced by factors like daylight exposure and weather.

Strategies for Navigating Energy Cycles

- **Work with Your Peaks:** Identify your personal energy peaks and schedule high-focus tasks during these periods.
- **Honor the Troughs:** Use low-energy periods for less demanding tasks like emails or administrative work.
- **Take Breaks:** Follow the ultradian rhythm by working intensely for 90 minutes and then resting for 10–15 minutes to recharge.
- **Seasonal Adjustments:** Adapt your routines to account for seasonal changes. For example, prioritize natural light exposure during winter months.

Actionable Tip:
Track your energy levels over a week, noting when you feel most and least motivated. Use this data to optimize your schedule.

Long-Term Strategies for Maintaining Motivation During Setbacks

Setbacks are inevitable on any journey, but they don't have to derail your motivation. Resilience and adaptability are key to maintaining energy and drive in the face of challenges.

1. Reframe Setbacks as Opportunities

- **Change the Narrative:** Instead of viewing setbacks as failures, see them as learning opportunities. Ask yourself, "What can I learn from this experience?"
- **Build a Growth Mindset:** Adopt the belief that abilities and success are not fixed but can be developed through effort and learning.

2. Use Reflective Practices

- **Journaling:** Write about your challenges and how you overcame similar obstacles in the past. This reinforces your resilience and provides clarity on how to move forward.
- **Gratitude Reflection:** Shift your focus to what's working well, helping to maintain a positive outlook.

3. Break Down Overwhelming Goals

- Large goals can feel daunting, especially during setbacks. Break them into smaller, actionable steps to regain momentum.
- Celebrate micro-successes to build confidence and motivation.

4. Stay Connected to Your "Why"

- Revisit the core reason behind your goals. When your purpose is clear and emotionally resonant, it becomes a powerful anchor during difficult times.
- **Visualization Exercise:** Imagine the long-term impact of achieving your goal and how it aligns with your values.

5. Seek Support

- Surround yourself with a supportive network of mentors, friends, or accountability partners. Share your challenges and lean on others for encouragement and guidance.

Building an Environment That Fuels Energy and Drive

Your environment significantly impacts your ability to sustain motivation and energy. A well-designed environment acts as a constant source of inspiration and support, while a poorly designed one can drain your energy and hinder progress.

Physical Environment

1. **Declutter and Organize:** A clean, organized space promotes mental clarity and focus.
2. **Designate Work Zones:** Create specific areas for focused work, relaxation, and creativity. This helps your brain associate each space with a specific activity.
3. **Incorporate Natural Elements:** Add plants, natural light, or calming colors to boost energy and reduce stress.

Social Environment

1. **Surround Yourself with Positive Influences:** Seek out individuals who inspire and uplift you. Avoid energy-draining relationships.
2. **Build a Motivation Circle:** Join communities or groups aligned with your goals. Shared accountability and encouragement can fuel long-term motivation.
3. **Limit Toxic Interactions:** Set boundaries with individuals or environments that consistently drain your energy.

Digital Environment

1. **Streamline Digital Tools:** Use apps and tools to organize your tasks, track progress, and minimize distractions.
2. **Set Digital Boundaries:** Limit time spent on social media or other activities that drain mental energy. Use focus apps or time limits to stay on track.
3. **Curate Inspiration:** Follow accounts, blogs, or channels that align with your goals and provide consistent motivation.

Rituals to Reinforce Energy

- **Morning Rituals:** Start each day with activities that energize and inspire you, such as exercise, meditation, or reading affirmations.
- **Evening Reflections:** End the day by reviewing accomplishments and setting intentions for the next day.
- **Weekly Recharge:** Dedicate time each week to activities that rejuvenate your mind, body, and spirit, such as hobbies, time in nature, or connecting with loved ones.

The Power of Consistency

Motivation and energy are not about perfection but consistency. By aligning your daily habits with your energy cycles, embracing setbacks as part of the journey, and building a supportive environment, you create a sustainable system that fuels long-term success.

Checklist for Sustaining Limitless Energy and Motivation

- **Track and optimize your energy cycles.**
- **Reframe setbacks as opportunities for growth.**
- **Stay connected to your "why" through regular reflection and visualization.**
- **Create an environment—physical, social, and digital—that supports your goals.**
- **Adopt rituals that recharge and refocus your energy daily and weekly.**

Sustaining limitless energy and motivation is a journey of self-awareness, adaptability, and intentional action. As you integrate these strategies into your life, you will discover that motivation becomes a constant force, empowering you to achieve your goals and maintain balance, even during challenges.

In the next chapter, we'll dive deeper into creating a long-term vision and aligning your goals with your energy and purpose, ensuring that your motivation not only endures but continues to grow. Let's move forward with clarity, confidence, and an unstoppable drive.

Appendix A: Quick Energy Boosters

Life doesn't always allow for a full recharge, but sometimes all you need is a quick energy boost to regain focus, motivation, and momentum. This appendix provides 20 actionable tips that can deliver an instant surge of energy. Whether you're feeling sluggish at work, drained after a long day, or simply need a mental reset, these techniques will help you feel revitalized in minutes.

1. Take 10 Deep Breaths

- **Why it works:** Deep breathing increases oxygen flow to the brain and calms the nervous system, improving focus and reducing stress.
- **How to do it:** Inhale deeply through your nose for 4 seconds, hold for 4 seconds, and exhale through your mouth for 6 seconds. Repeat 10 times.

2. Splash Cold Water on Your Face

- **Why it works:** Cold water stimulates the vagus nerve, which can increase alertness and reduce fatigue.
- **How to do it:** Rinse your face with cold water or use a damp, cold towel on your neck for an instant wake-up call.

3. Stretch It Out

- **Why it works:** Stretching releases tension in the body, improves circulation, and sends a signal to your brain to wake up.
- **How to do it:** Focus on stretches that open up your chest, shoulders, and hips, such as a standing forward fold or a gentle backbend.

4. Drink a Glass of Water

- **Why it works:** Dehydration is a common cause of fatigue. Rehydrating can quickly boost your energy.
- **How to do it:** Add a slice of lemon or a pinch of Himalayan salt to your water for an extra electrolyte boost.

5. Do 20 Jumping Jacks

- **Why it works:** Quick bursts of physical activity increase your heart rate, improve circulation, and release endorphins.
- **How to do it:** Stand with your feet together, arms at your sides. Jump, spreading your legs and raising your arms overhead, then return to the starting position.

6. Try a Power Pose

- **Why it works:** Standing in a confident posture can increase testosterone levels and reduce stress hormones, enhancing energy and confidence.
- **How to do it:** Stand tall with your feet apart, hands on your hips, and chest lifted. Hold the pose for two minutes.

7. Eat a Handful of Nuts or Seeds

- **Why it works:** Nuts and seeds like almonds, walnuts, or sunflower seeds provide healthy fats, protein, and magnesium for sustained energy.
- **How to do it:** Keep a small container of mixed nuts in your bag or desk for an easy snack.

8. Listen to an Energizing Song

- **Why it works:** Music with an upbeat tempo can instantly lift your mood and energy levels.
- **How to do it:** Create a playlist of your favorite high-energy songs to play whenever you need a pick-me-up.

9. Practice the "5-5-5" Technique

- **Why it works:** This mindfulness exercise resets your mental state by focusing your attention on the present moment.
- **How to do it:** Identify 5 things you can see, 5 things you can hear, and 5 things you can feel around you.

10. Eat a Piece of Dark Chocolate

- **Why it works:** Dark chocolate contains caffeine and theobromine, both of which boost energy and mood.
- **How to do it:** Choose dark chocolate with at least 70% cacao for maximum benefits.

11. Step Outside for Fresh Air

- **Why it works:** Exposure to sunlight and fresh air increases oxygen intake and stimulates the production of serotonin.
- **How to do it:** Spend 5–10 minutes outside, walking or simply standing in the sunlight.

12. Try Alternate Nostril Breathing

- **Why it works:** This breathing technique balances energy levels and calms the mind.
- **How to do it:** Close your right nostril with your thumb and inhale through your left nostril. Close your left nostril with your ring finger, open your right nostril, and exhale. Repeat for 2–3 minutes.

13. Drink Green Tea

- **Why it works:** Green tea provides a moderate caffeine boost without the crash, along with antioxidants to support energy production.
- **How to do it:** Sip slowly to enjoy its calming yet energizing effects.

14. Perform a Quick Desk Workout

- **Why it works:** Simple exercises like chair squats or desk push-ups get your blood flowing and combat sedentary fatigue.
- **How to do it:** Stand up from your desk and perform 10–15 squats or push-ups against your desk.

15. Snack on a Banana

- **Why it works:** Bananas are rich in natural sugars, potassium, and B vitamins, providing a quick energy boost.
- **How to do it:** Pair your banana with a tablespoon of almond or peanut butter for sustained energy.

16. Try Aromatherapy

- **Why it works:** Scents like peppermint, citrus, or eucalyptus can invigorate your senses and enhance focus.
- **How to do it:** Use an essential oil diffuser or rub a drop of oil onto your wrists and temples.

17. Chew a Piece of Gum

- **Why it works:** Chewing gum stimulates the brain and increases blood flow, improving alertness.
- **How to do it:** Choose a mint-flavored gum for an extra refreshing kick.

18. Do a Quick Meditation

- **Why it works:** A 3–5 minute meditation reduces mental clutter and resets your focus.
- **How to do it:** Close your eyes, breathe deeply, and focus on a single word or phrase, such as "energy" or "focus."

19. Incorporate a Superfood Boost

- **Why it works:** Superfoods like chia seeds, spirulina, or matcha provide nutrients that enhance energy and stamina.

- **How to do it:** Mix a teaspoon of chia seeds into water or add spirulina powder to a smoothie.

20. Laugh Out Loud

- **Why it works:** Laughter increases oxygen flow, reduces stress hormones, and releases endorphins.
- **How to do it:** Watch a quick funny video or recall a humorous moment to spark genuine laughter.

Final Thoughts

Quick energy boosters are valuable tools for maintaining momentum and combating fatigue. While they provide temporary surges, incorporating these techniques into your routine can also create long-term habits that enhance overall energy and motivation. Keep this list handy and experiment with different methods to discover what works best for you. With these strategies, you'll always have a way to recharge, refocus, and re-energize.

Appendix B: Tools and Resources for Energy Mastery

Mastering energy and motivation requires the right tools, resources, and strategies. This appendix provides a curated list of recommended apps, books, and tools to help you track and enhance your energy levels. Additionally, it includes templates to guide you in creating your personal energy and motivation plan, ensuring you can apply the concepts from this book effectively in your daily life.

Recommended Apps for Energy and Motivation

1. **Sleep Cycle (iOS, Android)**
   - **Purpose:** Tracks sleep patterns to help you wake up feeling refreshed.
   - **Key Features:** Smart alarm clock, detailed sleep analysis, and tips for improving sleep hygiene.
2. **Headspace (iOS, Android)**
   - **Purpose:** Enhances mental energy through guided meditation and mindfulness exercises.
   - **Key Features:** Focused meditation tracks for stress reduction, relaxation, and productivity.
3. **Forest (iOS, Android)**
   - **Purpose:** Boosts focus and mental energy by encouraging distraction-free work sessions.
   - **Key Features:** Gamified focus tracking where you grow a virtual tree by staying focused.
4. **WaterMinder (iOS, Android)**
   - **Purpose:** Helps maintain hydration levels to support physical energy.
   - **Key Features:** Customizable reminders to drink water, hydration tracking, and goal setting.

5. **MyFitnessPal (iOS, Android)**
   - **Purpose:** Tracks nutrition and activity to optimize physical energy.
   - **Key Features:** Calorie counting, macronutrient tracking, and fitness log integration.

6. **Habitica (iOS, Android)**
   - **Purpose:** Turns daily habits and tasks into a role-playing game to increase motivation.
   - **Key Features:** Task management, goal tracking, and rewards system to keep you engaged.

7. **Pomodoro Timer - Focus Booster (iOS, Android)**
   - **Purpose:** Improves productivity and mental energy by implementing the Pomodoro technique.
   - **Key Features:** Timed work sessions with short breaks, performance analytics.

8. **Strava (iOS, Android)**
   - **Purpose:** Tracks physical activity like running or cycling to maintain energy levels.
   - **Key Features:** GPS tracking, activity stats, and community challenges for motivation.

9. **Daylio (iOS, Android)**
   - **Purpose:** Tracks mood and energy levels over time to identify patterns.
   - **Key Features:** Journaling features, daily mood tracking, and visual trends analysis.

10. **Fabulous (iOS, Android)**
    - **Purpose:** Builds better habits for sustained energy and motivation.
    - **Key Features:** Habit coaching, goal-setting tools, and science-based daily rituals.

Recommended Books for Energy and Motivation

1. **"The Power of Habit" by Charles Duhigg**
   - Explores how habits are formed and provides actionable strategies to build energy-boosting habits.
2. **"Atomic Habits" by James Clear**
   - Offers a practical framework for creating habits that enhance motivation and energy.
3. **"Deep Work" by Cal Newport**
   - Focuses on maximizing productivity and mental energy through sustained focus and deep concentration.
4. **"The Energy Bus" by Jon Gordon**
   - A motivational fable that highlights the importance of positive energy and mindset in achieving success.
5. **"Why We Sleep" by Matthew Walker**
   - Explains the science of sleep and its impact on physical and mental energy.
6. **"Spark: The Revolutionary New Science of Exercise and the Brain" by John J. Ratey**
   - Demonstrates the link between physical activity and enhanced mental performance and motivation.
7. **"Mindset: The New Psychology of Success" by Carol S. Dweck**
   - Discusses the importance of a growth mindset in maintaining motivation and overcoming setbacks.
8. **"Eat Smarter" by Shawn Stevenson**
   - Provides insights into how nutrition impacts energy and brain function.

9. **"Drive: The Surprising Truth About What Motivates Us" by Daniel H. Pink**
   - Explores the science of motivation and how to cultivate it effectively.
10. **"The Miracle Morning" by Hal Elrod**
    - Outlines a morning routine designed to maximize energy, motivation, and productivity.

Recommended Tools for Enhancing Energy

1. **Standing Desk or Adjustable Desk**
   - Encourages movement throughout the day, reducing fatigue from prolonged sitting.
2. **Blue Light Blocking Glasses**
   - Reduces eye strain and improves sleep quality by minimizing blue light exposure in the evening.
3. **Aroma Diffuser with Essential Oils**
   - Scents like peppermint or citrus can boost alertness and energy.
4. **Resistance Bands**
   - Simple, portable equipment for quick, energy-boosting workouts.
5. **Fitness Tracker (e.g., Fitbit, Apple Watch)**
   - Tracks activity, heart rate, and sleep to optimize physical energy.
6. **Desk Timer or Productivity Clock**
   - Helps implement time management techniques like the Pomodoro method.
7. **Bullet Journal or Planner**
   - A tool for organizing tasks, tracking progress, and maintaining focus.
8. **Noise-Canceling Headphones**
   - Reduces distractions to enhance focus and mental energy.

Templates for Your Personal Energy and Motivation Plan
To help you integrate the strategies from this book, use the following templates to create your personalized energy and motivation plan.

Template 1: Daily Energy Planner

Time of Day	Energy Activity	Purpose	Outcome
Morning	Drink water, stretch	Kickstart physical energy	Refreshed and alert
Mid-Morning	Deep work session	Maximize mental energy	Task completed
Lunch Break	Light walk, healthy meal	Recharge physical energy	Rejuvenated for afternoon
Afternoon	Focused task with a break	Sustain productivity	Progress made
Evening	Gratitude journaling	Boost emotional energy	Positive mindset

Template 2: Weekly Energy Audit

Day	Energy Highs (When?)	Energy Lows (When?)	Activities to Adjust	Improvements for Next Week
Monday	10 AM, 3 PM	2 PM	Add a stretch break at 2 PM	
Tuesday				
...				

Template 3: Motivation Trigger Checklist

Trigger Type	Chosen Trigger	Associated Action/Goal	Effectiveness (1–10)
Physical (e.g., stretching)	10 push-ups	Start work on a big project	
Visual (e.g., image or quote)	Inspirational photo	Maintain focus on goal	
Auditory (e.g., music)	Motivational playlist	Energize for workout	

Template 4: Visualization and Affirmation Log

Date	Goal Visualized	Affirmation Used	Feelings/Results
January 1, 2024	Delivering a great speech	"I am confident and prepared."	Calm, motivated
January 2, 2024			

These tools and resources will help you track, enhance, and sustain your energy and motivation, ensuring that you stay aligned with your goals. Regularly updating your plans and reflecting on your progress will empower you to achieve peak performance and limitless motivation.

<u>Message from the Author:</u>

I hope you enjoyed this book, I love astrology and knew there was not a book such as this out on the shelf. I love metaphysical items as well. Please check out my other books:

-Life of Government Benefits

-My life of Hell

-My life with Hydrocephalus

-Red Sky

-World Domination:Woman's rule

-World Domination:Woman's Rule 2: The War

-Life and Banishment of Apophis: book 1

-The Kidney Friendly Diet

-The Ultimate Hemp Cookbook

-Creating a Dispensary(legally)

-Cleanliness throughout life: the importance of showering from childhood to adulthood.

-Strong Roots: The Risks of Overcoddling children

-Hemp Horoscopes: Cosmic Insights and Earthly Healing

- Celestial Hemp Navigating the Zodiac: Through the Green Cosmos

-Astrological Hemp: Aligning The Stars with Earth's Ancient Herb

-The Astrological Guide to Hemp: Stars, Signs, and Sacred Leaves

-Green Growth: Innovative Marketing Strategies for your Hemp Products and Dispensary

-Cosmic Cannabis

-Astrological Munchies

-Henry The Hemp

-Zodiacal Roots: The Astrological Soul Of Hemp

- Green Constellations: Intersection of Hemp and Zodiac

-Hemp in The Houses: An astrological Adventure Through The Cannabis Galaxy

-Galactic Ganja Guide

Heavenly Hemp

Zodiac Leaves

Doctor Who Astrology

Cannastrology

Stellar Satvias and Cosmic Indicas

Celestial Cannabis: A Zodiac Journey

AstroHerbology: The Sky and The Soil: Volume 1

AstroHerbology:Celestial Cannabis:Volume 2

Cosmic Cannabis Cultivation

The Starry Guide to Herbal Harmony: Volume 1

The Starry Guide to Herbal Harmony: Cannabis Universe: Volume 2

Yugioh Astrology: Astrological Guide to Deck, Duels and more

Nightmare Mansion: Echoes of The Abyss

Nightmare Mansion 2: Legacy of Shadows

Nightmare Mansion 3: Shadows of the Forgotten

Nightmare Mansion 4: Echoes of the Damned

The Life and Banishment of Apophis: Book 2

Nightmare Mansion: Halls of Despair

Healing with Herb: Cannabis and Hydrocephalus

Planetary Pot: Aligning with Astrological Herbs: Volume 1

Fast Track to Freedom: 30 Days to Financial Independence Using AI, Assets, and Agile Hustles

Cosmic Hemp Pathways

How to Become Financially Free in 30 Days: 10,000 Paths to Prosperity

Zodiacal Herbage: Astrological Insights: Volume 1

Nightmare Mansion: Whispers in the Walls

The Daleks Invade Atlantis

Henry the hemp and Hydrocephalus

10X The Kidney Friendly Diet
Cannabis Universe: Adult coloring book
Hemp Astrology: The Healing Power of the Stars
Zodiacal Herbage: Astrological Insights: Cannabis Universe: Volume 2
<u>**Planetary Pot: Aligning with Astrological Herbs: Cannabis Universes: Volume 2**</u>
Doctor Who Meets the Replicators and SG-1: The Ultimate Battle for Survival
Nightmare Mansion: Curse of the Blood Moon
<u>**The Celestial Stoner: A Guide to the Zodiac**</u>
Cosmic Pleasures: Sex Toy Astrology for Every Sign
Hydrocephalus Astrology: Navigating the Stars and Healing Waters
Lapis and the Mischievous Chocolate Bar

Celestial Positions: Sexual Astrology for Every Sign
Apophis's Shadow Work Journal: : A Journey of Self-Discovery and Healing
Kinky Cosmos: Sexual Kink Astrology for Every Sign
Digital Cosmos: The Astrological Digimon Compendium
Stellar Seeds: The Cosmic Guide to Growing with Astrology
Apophis's Daily Gratitude Journal

Cat Astrology: Feline Mysteries of the Cosmos
The Cosmic Kama Sutra: An Astrological Guide to Sexual Positions
Unleash Your Potential: A Guided Journal Powered by AI Insights
Whispers of the Enchanted Grove

Cosmic Pleasures: An Astrological Guide to Sexual Kinks

369, 12 Manifestation Journal

Whisper of the nocturne journal(blank journal for writing or drawing)

The Boogey Book

Locked In Reflection: A Chastity Journey Through Locktober

Generating Wealth Quickly:

How to Generate $100,000 in 24 Hours

Star Magic: Harness the Power of the Universe

The Flatulence Chronicles: A Fart Journal for Self-Discovery

The Doctor and The Death Moth

Seize the Day: A Personal Seizure Tracking Journal

The Ultimate Boogeyman Safari: A Journey into the Boogie World and Beyond

Whispers of Samhain: 1,000 Spells of Love, Luck, and Lunar Magic: Samhain Spell Book

Apophis's guides:

Witch's Spellbook Crafting Guide for Halloween

<u>Frost & Flame: The Enchanted Yule Grimoire of 1000 Winter Spells</u>

<u>The Ultimate Boogey Goo Guide & Spooky Activities for Halloween Fun</u>

Harmony of the Scales: A Libra's Spellcraft for Balance and Beauty

The Enchanted Advent: 36 Days of Christmas Wonders

Nightmare Mansion: The Labyrinth of Screams

Harvest of Enchantment: 1,000 Spells of Gratitude, Love, and Fortune for Thanksgiving

The Boogey Chronicles: A Journal of Nightly Encounters and Shadowy Secrets

The 12 Days of Financial Freedom: A Step-by-Step Christmas Countdown to Transform Your Finances

The Ultimate Black Friday Prepper's Guide: Mastering Shopping Strategies and Savings

Cosmic Sales: The Astrological Guide to Black Friday Shopping

Legends of the Corn Mother and Other Harvest Myths

Whispers of the Harvest: The Corn Mother's Journal

The Evergreen Spellbook

The Doctor Meets the Boogeyman

The White Witch of Rose Hall's SpellBook

The Gingerbread Golem's Shadow: A Study in Sweet Darkness

The Gingerbread Golem Codex: An Academic Exploration of Sweet Myths

The Gingerbread Golem Grimoire: Sweet Magicks and Spells for the Festive Witch

The Curse of the Gingerbread Golem

10-minute Christmas Crafts for kids

<u>Christmas Crisis Solutions: The Ultimate Last-Minute Survival Guide</u>

Gingerbread Golem Recipes: Holiday Treats with a Magical Twist

The Infinite Key: Unlocking Mystical Secrets of the Ages

Enchanted Yule: A Wiccan and Pagan Guide to a Magical and Memorable Season

Dinosaurs of Power: Unlocking Ancient Magick

Astro-Dinos: The Cosmic Guide to Prehistoric Wisdom

Gallifrey's Yule Logs: A Festive Doctor Who Cookbook

The Dino Grimoire: Secrets of Prehistoric Magick

The Gift They Never Knew They Needed

The Gingerbread Golem's Culinary Alchemy: Enchanting Recipes for a Sweetly Dark Feast

A Time Lord Christmas: Holiday Adventures with the Doctor

Krampusproofing Your Home: Defensive Strategies for Yule

Silent Frights: A Collection of Christmas Creepypastas to Chill Your Bones

Santa Raptor's Jolly Carnage: A Dino-Claus Christmas Tale

Prehistoric Palettes: A Dino Wicca Coloring Journey

The Christmas Wishkeeper Chronicles

The Starlight Sleigh: A Holiday Journey

Elf Secrets: The True Magic of the North Pole

Candy Cane Conjurations

Cooking with Kids: Recipes Under 20 Minutes

Doctor Who: The TARDIS Confiscation

The Anxiety First Aid Kit: Quick Tools to Calm Your Mind

Frosty Whispers: A Winter's Tale

The Infinite Key: Unlocking the Secrets to Prosperity, Resilience, and Purpose

The Grasping Void: Why You'll Regret This Purchase

Astrology for Busy Bees: Star Signs Simplified

The Instant Focus Formula: Cut Through the Noise

The Secret Language of Colors: Unlocking the Emotional Codes

Sacred Fossil Chronicles: Blank Journal

The Christmas Cottage Miracle

Feeding Frenzy: Graboid-Inspired Recipes

Manifest in Minutes: The Quick Law of Attraction Guide

The Symbiote Chronicles: Doctor Who's Venomous Journey

Think Tiny, Grow Big: The Minimalist Mindset

If you want solar for your home go here: https://www.harborso-lar.live/apophisenterprises/

Get Some Tarot cards: https://www.makeplayingcards.com/sell/
apophis-occult-shop

Get   some   shirts: https://www.bonfire.com/store/apophis-shirt-emporium/

<u>Instagrams:</u>
@apophis_enterprises,
@apophisbookemporium,
@apophisscardshop
Twitter: @apophisenterpr1
 Tiktok:@apophisenterprise
Youtube: @sg1fan23477, @FiresideRetreatKingdom
Hive: @sg1fan23477
CheeLee: @SG1fan23477

Podcast: Apophis Chat Zone: https://open.spotify.com/show/5zXbrCLEV2xzCp8ybrfHsk?si=fb4d4fdbdce44dec

Newsletter: https://apophiss-newsletter-27c897.beehiiv.com/

If you want to support me or see posts of other projects that I have come over to: **<u>buymeacoffee.com/mpetchinskg</u>**
I post there daily several times a day

Get your Dinowicca or Christmas themed digital products, especially Santa Raptor songs and other musics. Here: **https://sg1fan23477.gumroad.com**

Apophis Yuletide Digital has not only digital Christmas items, but it will have all things with Dinowicca as well as other Digital products.

www.ingramcontent.com/pod-product-compliance
Lightning Source LLC
Chambersburg PA
CBHW070559160726
48003CB00005B/2090